SUPER SANDCASTLE™

Animal Habitats

What Lives in the Forest?

Oona Gaarder-Juntti

Consulting Editor, Diane Craig, M.A./Reading Specialist

ABDO
Publishing Company

Published by ABDO Publishing Company, 8000 West 78th Street, Edina, Minnesota 55439. Copyright © 2009 by Abdo Consulting Group, Inc. International copyrights reserved in all countries. No part of this book may be reproduced in any form without written permission from the publisher. Super SandCastle™ is a trademark and logo of ABDO Publishing Company.

Printed in the United States.

Credits
Editor: Liz Salzmann
Content Developer: Nancy Tuminelly
Cover and Interior Design and Production: Oona Gaarder-Juntti, Mighty Media
Illustration: Oona Gaarder-Juntti
Photo Credits: AbleStock, Eyewire Images, iStockphoto/William Perry, Photodisc, ShutterStock

Library of Congress Cataloging-in-Publication Data

Gaarder-Juntti, Oona, 1979-

What lives in the forest? / Oona Gaarder-Juntti.

p. cm. -- (Animal habitats)

ISBN 978-1-60453-174-9

1. Forest animals--Juvenile literature. 2. Forest ecology--Juvenile literature. I. Title.

QL112.G23 2008

591.73--dc22

2008008204

Super SandCastle™ books are created by a team of professional educators, reading specialists, and content developers around five essential components— phonemic awareness, phonics, vocabulary, text comprehension, and fluency— to assist young readers as they develop reading skills and strategies and increase their general knowledge. All books are written, reviewed, and leveled for guided reading, early reading intervention, and Accelerated Reader® programs for use in shared, guided, and independent reading and writing activities to support a balanced approach to literacy instruction.

About SUPER SANDCASTLE™

Bigger Books for Emerging Readers
Grades K–4

Created for library, classroom, and at-home use, Super SandCastle™ books support and engage young readers as they develop and build literacy skills and will increase their general knowledge about the world around them. Super SandCastle™ books are part of SandCastle™, the leading PreK–3 imprint for emerging and beginning readers. Super SandCastle™ features a larger trim size for more reading fun.

Let Us Know
Super SandCastle™ would like to hear your stories about reading this book. What was your favorite page? Was there something hard that you needed help with? Share the ups and downs of learning to read. We want to hear from you! Send us an e-mail.

sandcastle@abdopublishing.com

Contact us for a complete list of SandCastle™, Super SandCastle™, and other nonfiction and fiction titles from ABDO Publishing Company.

www.abdopublishing.com • 8000 West 78th Street Edina, MN 55439 • 800-800-1312 • 952-831-1632 fax

Temperate forests get enough rain for trees, flowers, and shrubs to grow. The climate in the forest is warm in the summer and cold in the winter.

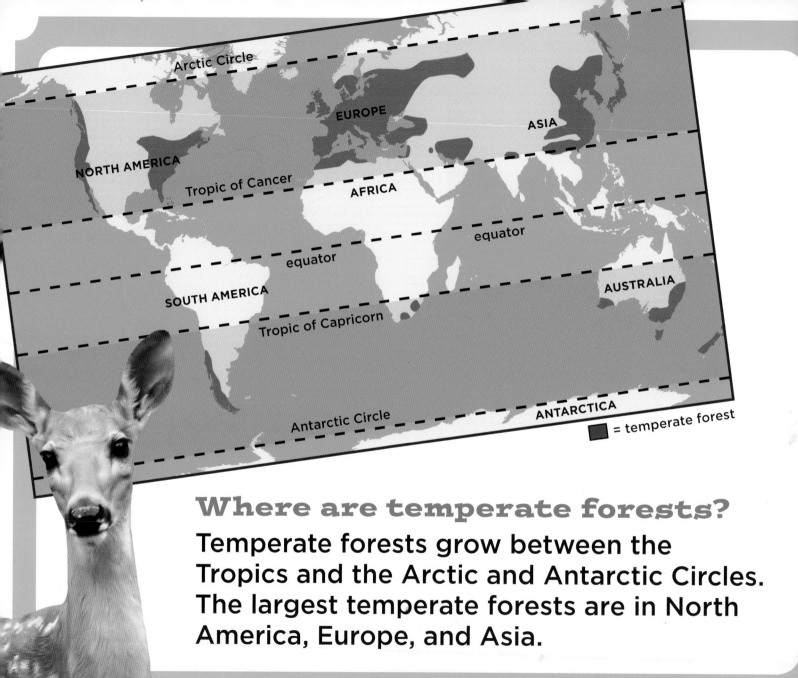

Arctic Circle

EUROPE

ASIA

NORTH AMERICA

Tropic of Cancer

AFRICA

equator

equator

SOUTH AMERICA

AUSTRALIA

Tropic of Capricorn

Antarctic Circle

ANTARCTICA

■ = temperate forest

Where are temperate forests?

Temperate forests grow between the Tropics and the Arctic and Antarctic Circles. The largest temperate forests are in North America, Europe, and Asia.

What do temperate forests look like?
The forest has five layers.

Tree Canopy

The tree canopy is the highest layer. The trees here are between 60 and 100 feet tall.

Small Tree

The small tree layer has shorter trees and young trees that are growing.

Shrub Layer

Smaller bushes grow in the shrub layer.

Herb Layer

Short plants and flowers grow in the herb layer.

Ground Layer

The forest floor gets very little sunlight. Moss grows here.

LUNA MOTH

Animal class: Insect
Location: North America

Luna moths have a wingspan of four to five inches. They have spots on their wings that look like eyes to confuse predators. Adult luna moths only live for a week.

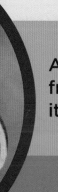

After a luna moth hatches from its cocoon, it has to let its wings dry before it can fly.

7

SPOTTED SALAMANDER

Animal class: Amphibian
Location: North America

Spotted salamanders live under rocks or logs, or in underground burrows. They come out at night to hunt for insects, worms, slugs, and spiders.

Female salamanders lay their eggs in ponds.

North American Porcupine

Animal class: Mammal
Location: North America

North American porcupines have more than 30,000 quills mixed in with their hair. A quill is a type of hair that is very sharp. Porcupines use the quills on their tails to defend themselves.

North American porcupines are good at climbing trees. They eat leaves, bark, nuts, small branches, and fruit.

BALD EAGLE

Animal class: Bird
Location: North America

The bald eagle is the national bird of the United States. Bald eagles live in forests near rivers, lakes, and wetlands. They can dive up to 200 miles per hour when hunting fish.

Bald eagles build large nests in treetops and on high cliffs. The largest nest ever found weighed more than two tons.

KOALA

Animal class: Mammal
Location: Australia

Koalas live in eucalyptus trees in Australia. They only eat eucalyptus leaves. Koalas move slowly and sleep up to 20 hours every day.

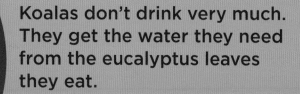

Koalas don't drink very much. They get the water they need from the eucalyptus leaves they eat.

Animal class: Mamma...
Location: Asia

Giant pandas live in ...
forests where bamboo shoots ...
They eat bamboo shoots a...
leaves. Pandas have large
back teeth and strong jaws
for chewing the tough
bamboo.

Giant pandas have enlarged
wrist bones that act like
thumbs. They help the
pandas hold their food.

17

MOUNTAIN LION

Animal class: Mammal
Location: North America and South America

Mountain lions are also known as pumas, cougars, panthers. They hunt at nig Mountain lions prey on dee coyotes, and porcupines

Mountain lions have hind legs. They can the ground to tree b 18 feet high.

MOOSE

Animal class: Mammal
Location: North America, Europe, and Asia

The moose is the largest deer species. Male moose have very large antlers. Their antlers can be six feet wide from tip to tip. Moose eat plants such as grass, leaves, and moss.

In the summer, moose eat water plants. They are good swimmers and can dive 18 feet underwater.

Have you ever been to a temperate forest?

More Temperate Forest Animals

Can you learn about these temperate forest animals?

black bear	rabbit
boar	raccoon
bobcat	red fox
cicada	red panda
collared peccary	skunk
coypu	squirrel
fox snake	white-tailed deer
goshawk	wild turkey
kookaburra	wombat
opossum	woodpecker

GLOSSARY

antler – a bony growth on the head of an animal in the deer family.

burrow – a hole or tunnel dug in the ground by a small animal for use as shelter.

canopy – a protective covering, such as an awning or high, leafy branches.

climate – the usual weather in a place.

defend – to protect from harm or attack.

eucalyptus – an Australian tree that is grown for its oil and wood.

female – being of the sex that can produce eggs or give birth. Mothers are female.

male – being of the sex that can father offspring. Fathers are male.

mammal – a warm-blooded animal that has hair and whose females produce milk to feed the young.

predator – an animal that hunts others.

shrub – a short plant with woody stems.

slug – a slimy creature that looks like a snail without a shell.

species – a group of related living beings.

wingspan – the distance from one wing tip to the other when the wings are fully spread.